# LAUNDRY AND BOURBON

### A COMEDY IN ONE ACT

### BY JAMES McLURE

★

★

DRAMATISTS
PLAY SERVICE
INC.

ELIZABETH CAULDER—Strong, sensuous woman. Intelligent but underdeveloped. Would be capable of handling most men other than Roy, her husband. Therein lies the attraction. A woman devoid of self-pity. A forthright person who would call your bluff.

HATTIE DEALING—A woman whose bluff needs calling. Blowsy, brassy, used to getting her own way. Mother, wife, talker. Has an adage for every occasion. Anything that has gone wrong in her life is Vernon's fault. Vernon is her husband.

AMY LEE FULLERNOY—Bright, sassy, spoiled. Baptist to the teeth. Given to gossip. Life revolves around the country club. An old enemy of Hattie's.

LAUNDRY AND BOURBON was presented by the McCarter Theater Company, Nagle Jackson, artistic director, at Princeton, New Jersey, in March, 1980, as part of a double bill with LONE STAR, under the omnibus title 1959 PINK THUNDERBIRD. It was directed by Mr. Jackson; the setting was by John Jensen; the lighting was by John McLain; and the costumes were by Michael J. Cesario. The cast, in order of appearance, was as follows:

| | |
|---|---|
| ELIZABETH | Ellen Tobie |
| HATTIE | Margo Martindale |
| AMY LEE | Leslie Geraci |

3

## THE SETTING: *THE CAULDER HOME.*

Facing the audience, the rear porch of a single-story, white, wooden frame house. There is a back door to the kitchen, flanked by two windows. Stage Right is a bedroom window, Stage Left a kitchen window.

It is a large deep back porch with a western exposure. From it one sees wide open pasture land, a hill, and the state highway beyond it. The road to the house from the highway is visible from the back porch although the road leads initially around to the front of the house.

The porch has railings on the side and a ceiling fan. There are two rocking chairs Stage Right, a low table in front of them. There is a pile of laundry waiting to be folded. Discarded magazines and papers lie around; it is obvious the porch hasn't been cleaned in days.

There is a sideboard Stage Left under the kitchen window. A black telephone is on the sideboard coming from the kitchen. Also on the sideboard is an old portable record player. Also Stage Left is a small kitchen table and one chair. A television set sits on a wooden crate either Downstage Left or Downstage Right.

## PRODUCTION NOTES

LAUNDRY AND BOURBON is the companion piece meant to precede my other play LONE STAR. In the playing of LAUNDRY AND BOURBON, the character of Elizabeth is intended to be the spiritual complement of Roy, the central character of LONE STAR. Therefore, Elizabeth should be played with a quality of great inner strength and character.

It is my intention that the two plays should be performed together to make a full evening in the theatre.

For convenience, depending upon the theatre, it is possible that Hattie and Amy Lee could make entrances from the front door through the house to the back porch, rather than around the side of the house as indicated.

4

# LAUNDRY
# AND BOURBON

AT RISE: *Elizabeth is smoking a cigarette, leaning against the porch post with a book in her arms. Music is playing on the phonograph. Doorbell rings. She doesn't move. Sound of Hattie kicking front door.*

HATTIE. (*Off.*) Elizabeth! Elizabeth. You in there. (*Voice getting closer.*) Where *are* you?

ELIZABETH. (*Resigned.*) I'm back here, Hattie. (*Hattie enters from around the side of the house, wearing a loud floral print dress.*)

HATTIE. Here you are. Is there something wrong with your doorbell.

ELIZABETH. I don't know.

HATTIE. I been ringing and ringing. Didn't you hear me *ring*?

ELIZABETH. Guess not.

HATTIE. Must be something wrong with your buzzer. Mmm?

ELIZABETH. I guess.

HATTIE. Your buzzer just don't buzz.

ELIZABETH. I'll have it checked. Come on in and sit a spell. (*Hattie steps onto porch.*)

HATTIE. A person could die out there in the heat. Just buzzing themselves to death. Buzz, buzz, buzz.

ELIZABETH. I'll have it checked.

HATTIE. Lord, it's like an oven out there. (*Pause.*) It's like an oven under here. Why don't we go inside where it's cool.

ELIZABETH. Can't the air conditioner's busted. Called Fuller-noy's. They're gonna send somebody out.

HATTIE. Lord. First your buzzer don't buzz, now your AC is on the blink. Looks like all your modern conveniences are just turning on you, girl. (*Hattie sits, fanning herself with a magazine.*)

ELIZABETH. Can I get you something.

HATTIE. No. I'm fine.

ELIZABETH. Coffee.

HATTIE. Nu-uh. I'm fine.

5

ELIZABETH. Ice tea.

HATTIE. Really. I'm fine.

ELIZABETH. Would you like some bourbon.

HATTIE. On the rocks with a splash of water. (*Elizabeth exits in kitchen.*)

ELIZABETH. You look beat.

HATTIE. I'm not beat, I'm in a frenzy.

ELIZABETH. What's the matter.

HATTIE. I'll wait'll you get back. I'm catching my breath.

ELIZABETH. Why you out of breath?

HATTIE. Mainly from buzzing your buzzer.

ELIZABETH. (*Irritated.*) I'll get it fixed. (*Elizabeth returns with drink.*) Here.

HATTIE. Thanks.

ELIZABETH. Nice dress Hattie.

HATTIE. Thanks, but it looked better on the mannequin than it does on me . . . Say where's that worthless husband of yours?

ELIZABETH. Roy?

HATTIE. No. Burt Reynolds. I noticed that his almighty Thunderbird wasn't out front.

ELIZABETH. Oh . . . he's in town about something.

HATTIE. Don't tell me he's actually gonna get a job.

ELIZABETH. Hattie. Don't start.

HATTIE. Okay. Okay. (*Pause.*) Say, you feel all right?

ELIZABETH. Yeah. Why.

HATTIE. I don't know you look kinda flushed.

ELIZABETH. Oh, it just must be the heat.

HATTIE. Yeah. Just must be the heat. (*Pause. Elizabeth takes a breath preparing for the performance she knows is coming. She enjoys playing straight man to Hattie.*)

ELIZABETH. So what're you in a frenzy about?

HATTIE. Oh yeah! Today I went through living hell.

ELIZABETH. What did you do?

HATTIE. (*Grimly.*) I went shopping with my children.

ELIZABETH. Bad, huh?

HATTIE. Disastrous. When my kids hit a department store they go berserk. I think it activates something in their glands. We hadn't been in J.C. Penney's five minutes before they scattered in all direction. Now you take my little Cheryl.

ELIZABETH. Uh-huh.

HATTIE. Now she's a sweet little thing but bless her heart she's a thief.

6

ELIZABETH. A thief.

HATTIE. It's time I faced facts, 'Lizabeth. My daughter is a kleptomaniac. As soon as we got into that store she started stuffing her pockets. Stuffing her clothing. She ran away from me and ten minutes later I saw her. I barely recognized my only daughter. She looked like a beach ball with legs.

ELIZABETH. Did you make her put it back?

HATTIE. Yes, but it does no good. Thieving is in her blood.

ELIZABETH. Where do you suppose she gets it?

HATTIE. From Vernon Jr.

ELIZABETH. Where was Vernon Jr. all this time?

HATTIE. He was in the hardware department.

ELIZABETH. Doing what?

HATTIE. Chasing his brother with a hammer.

ELIZABETH. Chasing little Roger?

HATTIE. Yes.

ELIZABETH. What was little Roger doing?

HATTIE. Screaming.

ELIZABETH. Oh Lord.

HATTIE. Oh Lord is right. And somehow Vernon Jr. broke a solid steel J.C. Penney hammer.

ELIZABETH. (*Laughing.*) How can you break a solid steel hammer?

HATTIE. Don't ask me. When it comes to destruction Vernon Jr. is a genius. But I tell you it's the last time I go shopping with those kids.

ELIZABETH. Where are the kids now?

HATTIE. I took the little darlings over to Vern's mother's place. She has a nice big house. (*Pause.*) They ought to have it levelled in about an hour or so. (*Sips. Elizabeth gets up, brings laundry over.*) What you doing?

ELIZABETH. Nothing. Just sit back and enjoy your drink. I've been putting this off all afternoon.

HATTIE. Here, I'll give you a hand.

ELIZABETH. Don't be silly.

HATTIE. Hush. I don't even have to think about it. I just put it on automatic pilot and fold. (*Pause. They fold in silence.*)

ELIZABETH. You don't have to be so particular with those T-shirts. Roy's got a jillion of them.

HATTIE. So does Vernon.

ELIZABETH. Why do men wear so many T-shirts.

HATTIE. I don't know.

7

ELIZABETH. I don't know either. (*Pause. Elizabeth stares blankly out at the land.*)

HATTIE. What you looking at.

ELIZABETH. Nothing.

HATTIE. (*Pause.*) You got a TV out here. (*Hattie gets up, moves to TV.*)

ELIZABETH. Yeah. It's an old one. I watch it out here some.

HATTIE. (*Checking watch.*) Ooooo. (*She turns on set.*)

ELIZABETH. What's on.

HATTIE. "Let's Make a Deal." (*Hattie returns to chair. Resumes folding without ever taking her eyes off the TV set.*)

ELIZABETH. OK, but keep the volume down. I can't stand to hear them women scream.

HATTIE. I know what you mean. (*Pause.*) All that yelling. (*Elizabeth goes back to work folding socks. Screaming.*) Oh! Would you look at that woman!

ELIZABETH. (*Startled.*) Where.

HATTIE. There! Would you do that!

ELIZABETH. Do what?

HATTIE. Dress up like a chicken!

ELIZABETH. Is that what that's supposed to be?

HATTIE. Of course it is. It's a chicken suit. The woman has dressed herself up like a chicken to be on national television.

ELIZABETH. That's stupid.

HATTIE. Of course it's stupid. (*Folds.*) Besides doesn't even look like a chicken. (*Folds.*) Chickens don't have bangs. (*Folds.*) Chickens don't have bangs. (*Folds.*) And I know. I've been around chickens all my life. (*They fold in silence. Screaming.*) Oh God!

ELIZABETH. What?

HATTIE. Look there, it's her husband.

ELIZABETH. So?

HATTIE. So! She's got him dressed like a rooster. Bad enough her dressed like a chicken, but to get a grown man dressed like a rooster!

ELIZABETH. (*Contemptuously.*) Huh! I could never get Roy to do that.

HATTIE. I should hope not. A man loses his masculinity when he's dressed up in a rooster suit. (*Pause. Transfixed. Glued to screen.*) Look. She can't make up her mind . . . what would you take? The curtain or the box?

ELIZABETH. The box.

8

HATTIE. Why?

ELIZABETH. "Good things come in small packages."

HATTIE. Wrong. Small things come in small packages.

ELIZABETH. Well, wedding rings come in small packages.

HATTIE. Yeah. But once you got one of them, honey, go for the big stuff.

ELIZABETH. She chose the curtain.

HATTIE. And it is? A dream vacation to British Honduras! Just think of it! British Honduras! (*Pause.*) Say, where is British Honduras?

ELIZABETH. South America, I think.

HATTIE. Why would any person want to go there?

ELIZABETH. Well she sure does. Look at her jump up and down. Looks like she's gonna wet her britches.

HATTIE. Well, she can relax. 'Cause she ain't going.

ELIZABETH. She just won it.

HATTIE. Well, she's gonna un-win it after this commercial.

ELIZABETH. You've seen this one before?

HATTIE. I've seen 'em all before.

ELIZABETH. How does she lose it?

HATTIE. The bitch gets greedy and goes for the grand prize.

ELIZABETH. Does she win?

HATTIE. No. She gets a year's supply of frozen meat pies.

ELIZABETH. (*Sadly.*) From British Honduras to frozen meat pies.

HATTIE. Yeah. Ain't fate weird. (*Pause. Fold.*)

ELIZABETH. Commercial's on. Want another drink? (*Elizabeth exits to fix drink.*)

HATTIE. Course I do. The main reason I come over here is to get away from the kids and get bombed. Lord you just don't know what it's like having a house full of kids.

ELIZABETH. No, I don't.

HATTIE. They're all the time underfoot. It's like living with midgets.

ELIZABETH. (*Elizabeth enters with drinks.*) You know I'll take them. Any time you need a rest.

HATTIE. Honey, couldn't do it. It'd give me a guilty conscience. (*Pause. They begin to fold a sheet together.*) How's everything? How's Roy?

ELIZABETH. Oh . . . you know Roy.

HATTIE. (*Grinning.*) Yeah, I know Roy.

9

ELIZABETH. (*Stopping her. Good-naturedly.*) Quit grinning. You don't know him that well.

HATTIE. I've known Roy all my life.

ELIZABETH. Yeah. But you didn't really get to know him till high school when you dated Wayne Wilder. We'd all go double-dating in Roy's Thunderbird.

HATTIE. Don't remind me.

ELIZABETH. (*Fondly.*) Why not? They were the most eligible boys in Maynard.

HATTIE. Nobody in Maynard is eligible.

ELIZABETH. Remember, we were all going to get married right after high school. Me and Roy. Wayne and you.

HATTIE. Yeah . . . but I ended up with Vernon Dealing.

ELIZABETH. Yeah. Isn't life funny?

HATTIE. Hilarious. (*Pause. Elizabeth crosses to TV.*) What're you doing?

ELIZABETH. I'm going to turn off the TV.

HATTIE. (*Restraining Elizabeth.*) No!! We haven't seen the grand prize!

ELIZABETH. But you already know what it is.

HATTIE. Yeah, but you don't.

ELIZABETH. But I don't want to know.

HATTIE. Sure you do! Quick, sit down. They're about to start. First they'll open curtain #2. Wait . . . wait. Aha. Frozen meat pies! And look there on old greedy's face. Yeah, she's trying not to act disappointed. Who you kidding, honey! You coulda been in British Honduras, missy. Not that it's very nice probably. Just one big jungle. But it sure beats hell outta frozen meat pies! *Now* . . . Curtain #1. An entire new kitchen and utility room ensemble. Big deal. Just look at that woman! Disappointment is carved on that face! If there's one thing no woman wants it's a new stove! Look! Look! Now she's crying and she wants us to think those are tears of joy! Baloney. You ain't gonna win no academy award with that performance.

ELIZABETH. Why do you watch this.

HATTIE. Elizabeth. TV game shows have everything. The thrill of victory, the agony of defeat! (*Slight pause.*) Mainly the agony of defeat.

ELIZABETH. Well, I think it's stupid.

HATTIE. What're you doing!

ELIZABETH. Turning it off.

HATTIE. Don't you want to know what the grand prize was.

10

ELIZABETH. No.

HATTIE. A brand new Lincoln Continental.

ELIZABETH. Who cares?

HATTIE. Well, you should. It's better than what you drive.

ELIZABETH. Roy's never gonna get rid of that Thunderbird.

HATTIE. He's had that car since high school.

ELIZABETH. He loves that car, Hattie.

HATTIE. What's so great about a 1959 pink Thunderbird convertible?

ELIZABETH. Roy says it's a classic.

HATTIE. It's a piece of junk.

ELIZABETH. (*Staring off.*) . . . Sometimes I think he loves that car more than me.

HATTIE. It's only a car.

ELIZABETH. Yeah, but he says it can take him where he wants to go.

HATTIE. That's stupid. (*Suspicious.*) Where does he want to go?

ELIZABETH. (*Almost to herself.*) I don't think he has any idea.

HATTIE. (*Puzzled.*) Well, good. Good. (*Pause.*) Well, we better get back to the laundry or we'll never get it done.

ELIZABETH. Oh, right. God I hate laundry.

HATTIE. Try doing it for three kids.

ELIZABETH. Week in. Week out. It's the same old clothes.

HATTIE. You can only look at so many pairs of Fruit of the Loom before you want to puke.

ELIZABETH. I'd like to burn everything in this basket and start all over. Everything except this shirt.

HATTIE. Why that shirt's all frayed.

ELIZABETH. It is now, but I remember the first time Roy wore this shirt.

HATTIE. When was that?

ELIZABETH. On our first date. He drove up in that pink Thunderbird in this shirt with all the pearl buttons. He looked just like Paul Newman in Hud. (*Hattie holds up a pair of boxer shorts.*)

HATTIE. God these shorts are big.

ELIZABETH. What?

HATTIE. These jockey shorts they're so big. They're not that wide. They're for a narrow body, but they're so long . . .

ELIZABETH. I suppose.

HATTIE. . . . Why're they so long.

ELIZABETH. Roy likes them big. Says he needs a lot of room. (*Pause.*)

11

HATTIE. Whew it's hot out here. (*Pause.*) Lordy, how's a body supposed to keep cool?

ELIZABETH. Nothing to do but fix a bourbon and coke and just sit and sweat.

HATTIE. I can't do that.

ELIZABETH. You can't sweat?

HATTIE. No. Fix a drink in the afternoon in front of the kids.

ELIZABETH. Why not?

HATTIE. Children learn by example.

ELIZABETH. So?

HATTIE. Well, all I need is to come home to a house full of kids sitting around drinking margueritas. You don't know what it's like raising a family.

ELIZABETH. No, I don't.

HATTIE. And lemme tell you, summertime is the worst.

ELIZABETH. What do you do?

HATTIE. I send them outside.

ELIZABETH. In this heat.

HATTIE. I give 'em a salt pill and say, play outside.

ELIZABETH. Don't they collapse from heat prostration?

HATTIE. Anything to slow them down.

ELIZABETH. I wish you'd let me take them sometimes.

HATTIE. Elizabeth you're not used to kids. The strain would kill you. (*Elizabeth moves D. Leans against porch post looking out over the land. Pause.*) Elizabeth, what are you staring out at that road for?

ELIZABETH. No reason. There's nothing to see.

HATTIE. That's the truth. Nothing green to look at. God, it's depressing living on the edge of a desert.

ELIZABETH. But just think millions of years ago all this land was under water.

HATTIE. Well . . . at least it would have been cool.

ELIZABETH. I like this land, but sometimes it gets too hot and burnt for people. It's still too wild and hard for anything to grow. (*Pause.*) Oh, look Hattie!

HATTIE. What is it?

ELIZABETH. Look at that cloud.

HATTIE. It's just a cloud.

ELIZABETH. Yeah, but look how it's throwing a shadow across the land. God, doesn't that shadow look peaceful gliding over the land. Doesn't it look cool? It reminds me of a cool dark hand

12

stroking a hot surface. (*Pause.*) Lately I've felt so hot and hollow inside I've wanted something to come along and touch me like that.

HATTIE. Elizabeth, what's the matter with you?

ELIZABETH. Nothing, Hattie, nothing.

HATTIE. (*Pause.*) You're doing it again, staring out at that hill. There ain't nothing out there but the highway and the road up to the house. Now, what're you expecting to see?

ELIZABETH. I was hoping to see a 1959 pink Thunderbird convertible come over that hill.

HATTIE. You've got tears in your eyes! Don't you tell me nothing's the matter! What is it? (*Pause.*)

ELIZABETH. Roy's been gone two days. (*Silence.*)

HATTIE. Why that son of a bitch! No wonder you've been so weird. Here, you sit yourself down here. I'm gonna fix you a drink and you're gonna tell me all about it.

ELIZABETH. I don't want another drink.

HATTIE. Hush up. Hattie's taking care of you now. The doctor is in. (*Elizabeth sits. Hattie exits to kitchen, talking.*) I knew there was something wrong the minute I laid eyes on you. First you didn't answer the doorbell, and as soon as I saw you I could tell something was the matter. That son of a bitch. (*Hattie returns, having mixed drinks in record time.*) Well, what brought it on this time?

ELIZABETH. I don't know. Things haven't been the same since he came back.

HATTIE. From Vietnam?

ELIZABETH. Yeah.

HATTIE. I know. I seen the change. But believe me you've been perfect about it.

ELIZABETH. I haven't been anything. I haven't done anything. He was the one that went off for two years. He was the one got shot up. He's the one that has nightmares.

HATTIE. Nightmares.

ELIZABETH. Yeah, almost every night. (*Pause.*) Anyway, now he's back and he can't seem to get nothing started. He made me quit the job at the pharmacy. He worked some out at his Dad's place. He's done some rough-necking out in the oil fields. But then always gets in fights and gets himself fired.

HATTIE. Well . . . what's he got to say for himself.

ELIZABETH. He says he's looking for something.

13

HATTIE. Hmnnn. What?

ELIZABETH. He doesn't know what. He says everything has changed here in Maynard.

HATTIE. Nothing's changed in Maynard since the Civil War.

ELIZABETH. I want him back the way it used to be.

HATTIE. Elizabeth, he's always been wild and unmanageable.

ELIZABETH. (*Flaring.*) I don't want to manage him. I don't want to break his spirit. That's why I married him, his spirit. Roy Caulder wasn't going to take no crap from anyone or anything. He and Wayne Wilder were gonna shake up the world.

HATTIE. Need I remind you that Wayne Wilder is currently serving five to ten for car theft?

ELIZABETH. (*Quietly.*) Roy's different than Wayne.

HATTIE. I wouldn't be too sure.

ELIZABETH. I just wished I knew he was safe. He could be hurt.

HATTIE. Or he could be with another woman.

ELIZABETH. I hope that's all it is.

HATTIE. Elizabeth, how can you say that?

ELIZABETH. Any man worthwhile is gonna look at other women. That's natural. And sometimes they wander a bit.

HATTIE. A bit? That man's done more wandering than Lewis and Clark.

ELIZABETH. You're exaggerating.

HATTIE. Last year? Last year! He took off for five days.

ELIZABETH. (*In spite of herself, smiling.*) Yeah. He had himself quite a time.

HATTIE. You mean he told you what he did?

ELIZABETH. Oh, sure.

HATTIE. Well, you never told me.

ELIZABETH. No.

HATTIE. But I'm your best friend. You're supposed to tell me everything.

ELIZABETH. It was different then. We'd had a fight and he left in a huff. Drove off to El Paso. Picked up a girl hitchhiking.

HATTIE. What was her name?

ELIZABETH. Hattie, how should I know? She was a hitchhiker.

HATTIE. A little tramp probably! A little hippie road slut! What's she look like?

ELIZABETH. Blonde.

HATTIE. A little blonde hippie bitch that never washed or nothing I'll bet!

ELIZABETH. Oh yeah, and there was one other thing . . .

HATTIE. What?

ELIZABETH. She had a tattoo.

HATTIE. A *tattoo* on her arm?

ELIZABETH. Not exactly on her arm.

HATTIE. God . . . where?

ELIZABETH. On her behind.

HATTIE. No! On her behind! How disgusting! . . . What did it say?

ELIZABETH. "Born to be wild."

HATTIE. Oh Lord! Lord!

ELIZABETH. Then Roy went down to El Paso got in a four-day poker game, won a hundred bucks and come on home.

HATTIE. Weren't you mad?!

ELIZABETH. Yes.

HATTIE. Didn't you want to shoot him?!

ELIZABETH. Yeah.

HATTIE. I would've.

ELIZABETH. I thought it was what he needed to get something out of his system. For a while it seemed to work. (*Pause.*)

HATTIE. Y'know half his trouble is that damn car of his.

ELIZABETH. What do you mean?

HATTIE. He gets behind the wheel of that car and he thinks he's the cock of the walk, the best-looking thing in these parts.

ELIZABETH. (*Proudly.*) He still is.

HATTIE. (*Grudgingly.*) Yeah.

ELIZABETH. Even the girls in high school today. I see them in town looking at him the way we did.

HATTIE. I never looked at him that way.

ELIZABETH. Hattie you still do.

HATTIE. I tell you it's that damn car. When he gets in it he thinks he's young and free again. (*Pause.*) Somebody ought to take that car away from him.

ELIZABETH. (*Warming to the memory.*) I remember the first day he drove into town in that car.

HATTIE. So do I.

ELIZABETH. He'd worked three years, summers and winters, for the down payment.

HATTIE. Only slightly used.

ELIZABETH. Roy and Wayne drove right through the center of town.

HATTIE. They looked like a couple of sultans.

ELIZABETH. It was bright pink.

HATTIE. It glistened like sin.

ELIZABETH. I remember I was coming out of the drug store with an ice cream cone.

HATTIE. What flavor.

ELIZABETH. Vanilla. And the sun off the hood was blinding. Couldn't even see the car. Then it passed into one shadow and I saw it. For the first time. It was beautiful, and Roy hardly knew me then but he waved at me, and I dropped my vanilla cone right there on the pavement. And I knew . . . he was the one.

HATTIE. Yeah. All through high school we double-dated.

ELIZABETH. Remember drive-ins, Hattie.

HATTIE. I sure do. More like wrestling matches.

ELIZABETH. One couple would get the car one night.

HATTIE. The other the next.

ELIZABETH. We'd drive around and drive around and then go make out.

HATTIE. Wayne and me didn't even drive around.

ELIZABETH. (*Rising.*) God, I want them back. I wished tonight was ten years ago. And Roy was coming to pick me up in that pink Thunderbird. I wished I could buy back some of the nights of summer I had in that car. When everything was cool and free and driving along the highway away from this stupid town. With the wind comirg at you and the stars all the way to the horizon, like diamonds that went all the way to dawn. (*Pause.*) Then driving off the road somewhere. By a lake maybe. Anywhere. Being off from town with the boy you loved better than anything ever in your whole life. I remember us making love for the first time. Really slow and gentle. God. He was gentle then. He taught me my body. I'd never really felt with my body before Roy. Suddenly it was like every pore of my skin was being opened like in a rain storm, feeling and holding everything you possibly wanted right there in your arms. What I wouldn't give to have those nights again. Just one night when the back seat of that Thunderbird was sweeter than all the beds in the world. (*Slight pause.*)

HATTIE. They took a lot of girls out in that car.

ELIZABETH. We were different.

HATTIE. Were we? (*They stare at each other.*) Look how he's treating you now. (*Pause.*) Elizabeth you're getting all sentimental and romantic. That happened to me once. I let a man run all over me.

ELIZABETH. What'd you do?

HATTIE. I wrote a poem.

ELIZABETH. You?

HATTIE. Yep. Worst afternoon of my life. Never do it again. That's what happens when you get all sentimental and miserable. You write poems. Just like old Emily Dickens.

ELIZABETH. Emily Dickinson.

HATTIE. That's the one. Poor gal was a miserable godforsaken old maid all her life and when she died all that was left was just a drawerful of poems.

ELIZABETH. What was your poem about, Hattie?

HATTIE. I wrote a poem about Wayne Wilder. He was a mean person and it was a mean poem. It was right after high school graduation. Wayne told me he was jilting me. You and Roy was getting married and Wayne Wilder was jilting me. Hit me like a ton of bricks. I went out back of the girls' gym, cried and wrote a poem. I still remember it.

"Oh Wayne you don't know, I love you so well
But you son of a bitch
I hope you roast in hell."

(*Pause.*) Not much of a poem, I guess. But then I decided to get practical like Hattie's always had to be. I went back to where everybody was in their caps and gowns and I saw Vernon Dealing standing there. He'd just been fiddlin' under some car hood. Even in his cap and gown his hands were dirty. But he was a good man and I knew he liked me. I got him to take me out. I got him to propose. Within a month we were married. Poor Vern. Never knew what hit him. (*Pause.*)

ELIZABETH. What are you telling me this for?

HATTIE. Roy's just like Wayne. He ain't never gonna change.

ELIZABETH. Maybe not.

HATTIE. I've known you all my life. I know you need a marriage and you want a family. Am I right.

ELIZABETH. Yes.

HATTIE. Then wake up. You can't leave the important things in life like marriage and children up to the menfolk. If they had their way they'd just stick to their football and their fishing and their Thunderbirds and just be boys forever. (*Pause.*) Now, if Roy straightens up, that's one thing. If not . . . well, you got to make a decision.

ELIZABETH. (*Privately.*) Maybe it's already been made for me.

HATTIE. What do you mean?

ELIZABETH. Nothing, Hattie. Forget I said that.

HATTIE. Don't tell me it's nothing . . . you're pregnant aren't you? (*Silence.*)

ELIZABETH. Yeah.

HATTIE. I knew it! I knew it the minute I walked in here today. Oh Elizabeth! That's wonderful!

ELIZABETH. What's wonderful about it? It comes at the worst possible time.

HATTIE. Wrong. It comes at the best possible time. Well, don't you see? This might be just the thing to make Roy straighten up and fly right.

ELIZABETH. And if it doesn't?

HATTIE. Then . . . to hell with him.

ELIZABETH. (*With difficulty.*) I guess . . . you're right.

HATTIE. Oh, honey! Let me give you a hug. That's the smartest thing you ever did.

ELIZABETH. (*Pulling away.*) What do you mean?

HATTIE. Getting pregnant, of course.

ELIZABETH. Hattie, I didn't get myself pregnant on purpose. I didn't plan it this way. (*Pause.*)

HATTIE. Are you sure.

ELIZABETH. (*Slightest hesitation.*) Yes! Yes, I'm sure. I don't know if Roy can take this right now. He doesn't know what he's doing himself.

HATTIE. Well, that's not your problem.

ELIZABETH. (*Angry.*) It's every bit my problem. It couldn't be any more my problem.

HATTIE. (*Pause.*) I didn't mean to get you all upset. I just meant . . .

ELIZABETH. (*Calmer.*) I know, Hattie, I know. I just don't want to talk about it anymore. (*Awkward pause.*)

HATTIE. Oh, well sure. Sure. Uh, say mind if I use your phone?

ELIZABETH. (*Smiling.*) Of course.

HATTIE. Figure I better check on the kids. No telling what devilment they've gotten up to. (*Dialing.*) Everything gonna turn out fine you'll see. (*On the phone.*) Hello? Cheryl? Cheryl dear, this is Mommy . . . Mommy . . . *your mother.* (*Aside.*) Child needs a hearing aid. What's that dear? Vernon Jr. threw a rock at you? Well, throw one back at him, honey. Show him who's boss. Cheryl, sweetheart, put Grandma on the phone . . . Cheryl this week!

(*Pause.*) Sounds like they're running her ragged. Hello? Little Roger. Is that you. I don't want to talk to you right now punkin, I want to talk to Grandma . . . 'cause I want to talk to Grandma . . . yes Grandma does have baggy elbows. Now lemme talk to her . . . what's that? Honey of course Mommy loves you . . . I love you all the same . . . Do I love you more than who? Fred Flintstone. Yes. More than Paul Newman no, but Fred Flintstone yes . . . It's a grown-up joke honey. Now put Grandma on . . . She's what? Tied up! You untie her you hear me? You want a switchin'? . . . Then you untie her, right now . . . Marion? That you . . . Oh, you were playin' . . . Oh good I thought they had you tied up for real . . . How they doing . . . yes . . . yes . . . yes I agree there is too much violence on TV . . . yes I'll pick them up at five . . . No I won't be late . . . You have my solemn word . . . Goodbye. What's that? Little Roger? . . . Yes it's nice to hear your voice again too . . . You're playing what? Sniper? Vernon Jr. has climbed a tree in the backyard and he has a brick? Well, little Roger, listen and listen carefully, under no circumstances go under that tree . . . He's gonna drop the brick on your head, sweetheart . . . So don't go under the tree. That's just what he wants . . . OK . . . OK . . . "Yabba dabb doo" to you too. (*She hangs up.*) He'll walk right under that tree. The child has no more sense than God gave a screwdriver.

ELIZABETH. What's abba dabba doo?

HATTIE. Yabba dabba doo. That's what Fred Flintstone says when he's happy. (*We hear the sound of Elizabeth setting her drink down on the counter and gasping.*) Elizabeth, what's the matter?

ELIZABETH. There. There's a car coming up the road.

HATTIE. Is it Roy?

ELIZABETH. I can't tell . . . no. No.

HATTIE. Who could it be? You expecting someone?

ELIZABETH. No.

HATTIE. Isn't that just the way? Here you are all pregnant and depressed and people are dropping in unannounced.

ELIZABETH. Wait. I did call up Fullernoy's about the air conditioning.

HATTIE. Oh my God!

ELIZABETH. What?

HATTIE. That's who it is! Amy Lee Fullernoy!

ELIZABETH. Well, I asked them to send somebody out, but I

didn't think they'd send Amy Lee. (*A flurry of activity begins. Elizabeth begins straightening up the porch. All the carefully folded clothes get thrown helter-skelter into the laundry basket. Magazines, newspapers, are collected. As Elizabeth straightens up, she neglects the "long" pair of Roy's underwear on the table R. Hattie busies herself with fixing her make-up.*)

HATTIE. Of course not. What does Amy Lee Fullernoy know about fixing air conditioners?

ELIZABETH. I don't know.

HATTIE. Not a damn thing. I wonder what she wants? (*Pause.*) Are you friends with her all of a sudden?

ELIZABETH. Of course not.

HATTIE. Good, 'cause you know our bridge club isn't speaking to her bridge club.

ELIZABETH. I know, and I think it's ridiculous.

HATTIE. Of course it is, but they started it. Theirs is practically the only other game in town. If we combined groups we'd have better games. We could have teams, tournaments. We could have round robins, goddamit! But no they won't play with us.

ELIZABETH. (*Weary.*) That's not true. Amy Lee and her group belong to the country club. That's where they play their games. We can't play there on a regular basis 'cause we don't belong. Those are the rules.

HATTIE. Well, they're dumb rules.

ELIZABETH. But it's like Amy Lee says, "What's the point of a country club if you can't keep people out."

HATTIE. Well, I agree with her. Keep *some* people out. But why does it have to be me?

ELIZABETH. Well, join the damn thing then if it means that much to you

HATTIE. You better believe I am! As soon as I get Vernon off his ass and making some more money. Lord, that man's hard to motivate. It's like pulling a mule through mud. (*Doorbell rings. Elizabeth begins to answer. Hattie stops her. Pouting.*) Don't answer it.

ELIZABETH. Why?

HATTIE. Because it's Amy Lee Fullernoy.

ELIZABETH. That's no excuse.

HATTIE. She'll ruin our afternoon. (*Doorbell.*)

ELIZABETH. Let go of my arm, Hattie.

HATTIE. Amy Lee is so tacky. She thinks she's cute, but she's tacky.

ELIZABETH. Quit being silly and let me go.

HATTIE. I wonder who picks out her wardrobe? Ray Charles. (*Hattie laughs with a snort.*) Ray Charles! Get it.
ELIZABETH. I got it. (*Exiting.*) Hold on Amy Lee, I'm coming. (*Elizabeth exits. Hattie still enjoying herself.*)
HATTIE. Ray Charles. That was a good one! (*Heard in the front room: "Elizabeth," "How are you?" "Amy Lee, c'mon in" . . . etc.*) God I hate Amy Lee. (*Amy Lee enters with Elizabeth, carrying a large box, unmarked, and wearing a dress exactly the same as Hattie's. Hattie turns to greet Amy Lee.*) Amy Lee!
AMY LEE. Hattie!
HATTIE and AMY LEE. Girl, how are youuuuuuuuuu! (*Silence.*)
HATTIE. I can't believe it.
AMY LEE. Oh no. (*Elizabeth steps in between Hattie and Amy Lee.*)
ELIZABETH. Why, Hattie, your new dress looks a lot like Amy Lee's doesn't it?
HATTIE. That's 'cause it's the exact same dress.
ELIZABETH. You two must have the same designer. Who is it Hattie? Mr. Charles wasn't it?
HATTIE. Yes, Mr. Charles.
AMY LEE. Mr. Charles? Who's he?
HATTIE. Frenchman. Lives in Dallas. (*Pause.*) Anyway . . . it looks real nice on you, Amy Lee.
AMY LEE. Oh yours does too.
HATTIE. (*Pause.*) God, I feel like a bookend.
ELIZABETH. Can I get you anything.
AMY LEE. I can only stay a minute. I've something in the oven that'll burn if I don't get back.
ELIZABETH. You sure.
HATTIE. Oh stay.
AMY LEE. Well . . . what were you two having?
HATTIE. Oh, just a little highball.
AMY LEE. A highball?
HATTIE. It's a drink.
ELIZABETH. Hattie, Amy Lee's a Baptist.
HATTIE. Sorry.
AMY LEE. Oh now I take a drink every now and then. I'm just a backporch Baptist.
ELIZABETH. Would you like a bourbon and coke.
AMY LEE. Just a wee one.
HATTIE. Thatta girl. (*Elizabeth exits. Hattie stares at the box.*) My what a big box. Have you been shopping?

AMY LEE. (*Smiling.*) Oh no. (*Pause.*)

HATTIE. (*Smiling.*) Still it's an awfully *big* package.

AMY LEE. Yes it is.

HATTIE. Yes sir. (*Pause.*) Sure is a big box.

ELIZABETH. (*In background.*) What have you been up to Amy Lee.

AMY LEE. Been busy as a bee. I'm on the entertainment committee for the country club, and the recreation committee for First Baptist.

HATTIE. That sounds tough.

AMY LEE. It is. Because there's very few fun things a Baptist can do without risking damnation.

HATTIE. And the country club committee too?

AMY LEE. I *am* the entertainment committee.

HATTIE. No one to help you?

AMY LEE. Clara Simms.

HATTIE. I see what you mean.

AMY LEE. One can't expect many clever ideas from a woman that's had two strokes in one year.

HATTIE. No.

AMY LEE. No. (*Pause.*) I love the way you're wearing your hair, Hattie.

HATTIE. Yes?

AMY LEE. Yeah. It's just as cute as a bug.

HATTIE. Cute as a *bug*?

AMY LEE. I mean button. Cute as a button. (*Pause.*) Elizabeth, how's Roy?

ELIZABETH. Roy? Roy's fine, Amy Lee.

AMY LEE. Oh I'm so glad to hear it!

ELIZABETH. How's Cletis!

AMY LEE. Oh. He's doing *so* well. So well at the store. Cletis is so funny. I have to keep a short rein on him though or he'd just overstock everything.

HATTIE. Well we wouldn't want that to happen.

AMY LEE. No indeed.

HATTIE. Lord, this is a big box, Amy Lee. (*Pause.*)

AMY LEE. (*Laughing.*) Honey quit worrying about that box. (*Pause.*) Well, Hattie, what have you been doing with yourself?

HATTIE. Honey, keeping up with three kids is a full-time job.

AMY LEE. Cletis and I, of course, want children . . .

HATTIE. Uh-huh.

AMY LEE. I'm just *dead* for some, but I don't want to be tied down just yet. Children can be such a lot of trouble.

HATTIE. (*Expertly.*) Well, of course they can be if they do not receive proper disciplinary guidance. Children must be taught.

AMY LEE. I'm sure you are aware of the problems since your children are so . . . high-spirited themselves.

HATTIE. Yes, but well-behaved. Now you take my little Cheryl. A perfect angel.

AMY LEE. What about Vernon Jr.

HATTIE. And little Roger is adorable! He's so quiet. For the first month we thought he was deaf.

AMY LEE. And Vernon Jr.?

HATTIE. (*Darkly.*) What about him?

AMY LEE. My neighbors, the Burns, had some trouble with Vernon.

HATTIE. You friends with the Burns?

AMY LEE. I'm neighborly with them. But never friendly. I don't want them to get the wrong impression.

HATTIE. So one of their kids played with Vernon?

AMY LEE. Yes, he's just now getting out of the cast.

HATTIE. What's his name?

AMY LEE. Chester Burns.

HATTIE. I know the Burns boy. A born liar. (*Phone rings. Elizabeth answers.*)

ELIZABETH. Hattie, it's for you.

HATTIE. (*Rising.*) His father was a liar too! Bobby Burns. 'Member? We went to grade school with him. "Lie-a-minute Burns" we used to call him. Excuse me.

AMY LEE. Of course. (*Elizabeth and Hattie in doorway. Elizabeth with phone. Phone sits on kitchen counter inside doorway.*)

ELIZABETH. It's Marion.

HATTIE. Are the kids acting up?

ELIZABETH. Something about a bonfire.

HATTIE. (*Gaily.*) Hello. Marion? What's the matter, honey? Why're you coughing? Do you have a cold . . . Oh. That much smoke huh . . . Well turn on the fan . . . How're the kids . . . They did what? . . . Oh, no they wouldn't do that to Poochie . . . They love that dog . . . At least they wouldn't do it on purpose . . . Yes . . . yes . . . Well, you know Poochie's a pekinese and they have long hair . . . They catch on fire easily . . . Well . . . Yes . . . Well . . . Marion, look it coulda

been worse . . . It was just the tail . . . (*The phone goes dead.*
*Obviously Marion has hung up. Elizabeth enters with tray of drinks,*
*crackers, cheese, etc.*)
ELIZABETH. What was all that about?
HATTIE. Oh, Marion's dog, Poochie's tail caught on fire. She's
trying to frame my children. (*To Amy Lee.*) She's overprotective
about that animal.
AMY LEE. Well, would you just look at all this?
ELIZABETH. It's nothing.
HATTIE. It looks real nice, Elizabeth.
ELIZABETH. It's only crackers and dip. What brings you out
this way, Amy Lee?
AMY LEE. Just to visit.
ELIZABETH. Uh-huh . . .
AMY LEE. And to do some business.
HATTIE. Uh-huh.
AMY LEE. (*Cheerfully.*) Girls! It's that time of year again at First
Baptists!
ELIZABETH. Not . . . pancake supper?
AMY LEE. You guessed!
HATTIE. How much are the tickets?
AMY LEE. Five dollars.
HATTIE. That's a lot to pay for a stack of flapjacks.
AMY LEE. All the proceeds go to charity.
HATTIE. Last year they were leathery. Made me sick.
AMY LEE. Our mission in Paraguay has worked wonders.
HATTIE. Paraguay? Where's that?
AMY LEE. South America. It's a very backward country.
HATTIE. No wonder it's backward. Only people there are people
from game shows and Baptists.
AMY LEE. What?
ELIZABETH. Never mind.
AMY LEE. Anyway. There are souls need saving there. The
people are starving to death. We bring them Jesus.
ELIZABETH. If they're starving, why don't you bring them a hot
meal?
AMY LEE. Oh, we do. All sorts of good things.
ELIZABETH. Like what?
AMY LEE. Powdered milk. Instant eggs.
HATTIE. Um. Yummy.
AMY LEE. The underdeveloped countries need the Blood of the
Lamb.

HATTIE. Blood of the Lamb?

AMY LEE. Yes. The forgiveness of God. The compassion of Christ. Christian charity. And we gotta hurry, 'cause the Catholics got a head start on us.

ELIZABETH. Frankly, I say let them have it.

AMY LEE. Elizabeth! Communism flourishes in Catholic countries! You were raised Methodist. That's practically Baptist. You ought to know that!

ELIZABETH. Well, I don't.

AMY LEE. Hattie, how were you raised?

HATTIE. With a stick.

AMY LEE. Oh that's right.

HATTIE. Spare the rod and spoil the child.

AMY LEE. I forgot your people are from Mississippi.

HATTIE. Yes. They were in agriculture.

AMY LEE. Anyway. In many Catholic countries, Protestant missions are the only thing standing between us and the Red threat!

ELIZABETH. Lord, Amy Lee. It sounds like you've joined the John Birch Society.

AMY LEE. Honey, I can't. I'm involved in too much club work as it is. (*Elizabeth goes to get purse. Hattie digs checkbook out of purse. Amy Lee produces a roll of tickets.*)

ELIZABETH. Here's my five.

AMY LEE. Think of this as a contribution to the Kingdom of Heaven.

HATTIE. Will the Kingdom of Heaven take a check?

AMY LEE. (*Continuing.*) Uh-huh. A contribution to a better world. And isn't that what we all want for our children? As mothers. And mothers-to-be?

HATTIE. Don't worry Amy Lee. You're a real mother already. (*Hattie rips out a check. Amy Lee rips off a ticket. They exchange. Pause.*) Excuse me. I've got to go to the little girl's room. (*Pause as she exits.*)

ELIZABETH. Hattie's had a few.

AMY LEE. I never listen to Hattie when she's talking like a sharecropper's daughter. (*Smiles.*) Which she is.

ELIZABETH. What's in the box?

AMY LEE. What box?

ELIZABETH. That box.

AMY LEE. Oh! I'd forget my head if it wasn't screwed on. It's the air filter.

ELIZABETH. What air filter?

AMY LEE. For your air conditioner.

ELIZABETH. Don't need one.

AMY LEE. What? Cletis told me you did.

ELIZABETH. My filter's fine. It's the motor. Damn thing won't turn on.

AMY LEE. Oh.

ELIZABETH. Yes.

AMY LEE. Well, Cletis told me y'all talked and he said it might be your air filter, so I decided to run one out.

ELIZABETH. No. (*Pause.*) Didn't talk to Cletis.

AMY LEE. Oh?

ELIZABETH. No. Talked to James.

AMY LEE. (*Recovering.*) Oh that's right! Cletis told me James had taken the order and said it sounded like it might be your filter. So I decided to run one out.

ELIZABETH. Oh. Well bless your heart. (*Her smile vanishing.*) What do you need here, Amy Lee? (*Silence. Hattie returns. Immediately notices the box has been moved.*)

HATTIE. Where's the box?

AMY LEE. There.

HATTIE. Oh. Thank God. (*Smiling.*) Didn't want you to lose it. (*Hattie sits. She immediately notices the hostility in the air.*)

AMY LEE. (*Nervously.*) Soooo . . .

HATTIE. Yeah? Soooo . . .

AMY LEE. How have you been, Hattie?

HATTIE. (*Wary.*) Fine.

AMY LEE. (*Overly sincere.*) I'm *so* glad. How's Vernon?

HATTIE. (*Begins to answer, then—*) Well he's—you never ask about Vernon! What the hell's going on here? What have you two been talking about? Have you two been talking about me? God! I leave the room and people talk about me! I'm an object of gossip!

ELIZABETH. No. We haven't been talking about you Hattie.

HATTIE. Well good. Good.

ELIZABETH. No. But I think Amy Lee was about to tell me something.

AMY LEE. (*Embarrassed.*) Well, Elizabeth . . .

ELIZABETH. Go on Amy Lee.

HATTIE. Yeah. What is it?

AMY LEE. Well . . . not in front of Hattie.

HATTIE. What do you mean not in front of Hattie?! Anything you can say to her you can say to me.

ELIZABETH. Go on Amy Lee.

26

AMY LEE. (*Pause.*) Well . . . it's about Roy.

ELIZABETH. What about Roy?

AMY LEE. It pains me to say this . . .

HATTIE. I bet.

AMY LEE. I saw Roy yesterday . . .

ELIZABETH. (*Covering.*) Really? Where?

AMY LEE. Here in Maynard.

ELIZABETH. And . . .

AMY LEE. Well, he wasn't alone.

ELIZABETH. Who was he with?

AMY LEE. It pains me to say this . . .

ELIZABETH. Force yourself.

AMY LEE. Margaret Crowell.

HATTIE. (*Quietly.*) Margaret Crowell?

AMY LEE. Yes. (*Hattie takes a long sip of her drink.*)

ELIZABETH. Thank you Amy Lee.

AMY LEE. I thought you should know.

ELIZABETH. Thank you.

AMY LEE. I thought you should hear it from someone who cares. (*Pause.*) I'm sorry.

ELIZABETH. Why?

AMY LEE. (*Confused.*) Well, because . . .

ELIZABETH. Nothing to be sorry about. I knew Roy was with Margaret Crowell.

AMY LEE. You did?

HATTIE. You did?

ELIZABETH. Yeah. He called yesterday. He was late for supper. He called and said he'd given Margaret Crowell a lift.

AMY LEE. Oh Elizabeth . . .

HATTIE. You see there!

AMY LEE. I feel terrible!

HATTIE. You ought to!

AMY LEE. I feel horrible!

HATTIE. People like you start rumors!

ELIZABETH. It's OK, Amy Lee.

HATTIE. Vicious tongues!

AMY LEE. (*Standing.*) You want me to go. I know you do.

ELIZABETH. Sit down.

AMY LEE. How can you stand to look at me?

HATTIE. It's not easy.

ELIZABETH. Sit down I'll fix you a drink.

HATTIE. (*Sweetly.*) Let me fix it.

AMY LEE. Elizabeth, can you forgive me?

ELIZABETH. I forgive you, Amy Lee.

AMY LEE. Oh, you're a Christian soul. Isn't she a Christian soul?

HATTIE. (*Pouring a huge drink at sideboard.*) Hell, we're all Christian souls. (*Hattie pours Amy Lee an enormously potent drink.*)

AMY LEE. Elizabeth, I feel so bad.

ELIZABETH. Forget it.

AMY LEE. So many bad marriages lately in Maynard has made me unnaturally suspicious.

HATTIE. What do you mean? (*Hattie returns with the drink.*)

AMY LEE. The American family's just falling apart!

HATTIE. Cheers!

AMY LEE. Cheers!

ELIZABETH. Cheers. (*They all drink.*)

AMY LEE. Whew that's strong.

HATTIE. The second sip is always smoother.

AMY LEE. (*Sipping, then smiling brightly.*) You're right.

HATTIE. Now, what's all this about bad marriages?

AMY LEE. Well, Maynard, Texas has just become another Peyton Place, that's all.

HATTIE. Well, tell.

AMY LEE. Well people are just running around on each other.

HATTIE. Well who?

AMY LEE. Laurette Weems.

HATTIE. Who would run around with Laurette Weems.

AMY LEE. No. Her husband's been running around on her.

HATTIE. I don't blame him.

AMY LEE. This is her third marriage.

HATTIE. It sure is.

AMY LEE. Yes, there's something seriously wrong in Laurette's approach to modern marriage.

HATTIE. Who else.

AMY LEE. Dorthea Hicks is expecting.

HATTIE. What do you expect? She's Catholic.

AMY LEE. But six children.

HATTIE. She doesn't have children. She drops litters. (*Amy Lee shares a dirty laugh with Hattie.*) Who else.

AMY LEE. Jenny Jo Gilcrease.

HATTIE. Divorced?

AMY LEE. Pregnant.

HATTIE. No! They can't afford that child.

AMY LEE. Of course not.

HATTIE. What does her husband do?

AMY LEE. Works at the amusement park over in Snyder. Runs the go-cart ride.

HATTIE. *Oh brother.*

AMY LEE. But you want to hear the best part.

HATTIE. What.

AMY LEE. He doesn't want the child!

HATTIE. Oh no!

AMY LEE. Yes! She told me that he told her that if she got pregnant that was her tough luck. She could just raise it herself.

HATTIE. That man has no sense of responsibility.

AMY LEE. But listen to this.

HATTIE. There's more?

AMY LEE. Do you know what Jenny Jo is contemplating?

HATTIE. What?

AMY LEE. Abortion.

HATTIE. Abortion?

AMY LEE. Yes m'am.

HATTIE. Nooooo . . .

AMY LEE. Where she'd get it I don't know. She can't get one in Maynard. She'd have to go to some place that didn't have any morality. Like Dallas or Houston.

ELIZABETH. But can you imagine her position?

HATTIE. She shouldn't have gotten herself pregnant by a man who raced go-carts.

AMY LEE. (*Virtuous.*) Hattie, you're being heartless.

HATTIE. Hattie's just telling it like it is. (*Right at Amy Lee.*) I know plenty of people who've married for money.

ELIZABETH. (*Angry.*) I wished you could hear yourselves.

AMY LEE. Why.

HATTIE. What's up?

ELIZABETH. So Jenny Jo has gone and gotten herself pregnant. What business is it of yours. So her husband doesn't want it? What business is it of yours? She probably told you all that 'cause she had nobody else to listen to. Somebody she could open up to. God, don't you know she feels like the loneliest person in the world.

HATTIE. (*Pause.*) Elizabeth, you're right. I'm sorry.

AMY LEE. Yeah. We shouldn't have picked on that poor pregnant Catholic girl like that.

ELIZABETH. (*Embarrassed.*) Uhmm . . . Sorry. I don't know what got into me there. I didn't mean to spoil the party. Here have some dip.

AMY LEE. This is good dip.

ELIZABETH. Fresh avocadoes. I grow 'em myself out in the garden. (*Pause. Amy Lee mistakes the "long" pair of Roy's underwear, which Elizabeth neglected to remove from the coffee table, for a table napkin. She demurely wipes her mouth with the underwear. They all realize what it is at the same time and break up. As the laughter subsides, Elizabeth gamely tries to get the conversation back to a polite level.*) Well, Amy Lee, so how's your bridge game, girl.

AMY LEE. (*With elaborate boredom.*) Oh that. It's fine.

HATTIE. Don't tell me you've given up bridge.

AMY LEE. Well, no.

HATTIE. Thank heavens. It took me forever to learn bridge.

AMY LEE. But in just a few months I doubt whether anyone will be playing bridge at all.

HATTIE. (*Panic.*) What!?

AMY LEE. You mean you haven't heard the news.

HATTIE. News? What news?

AMY LEE. Haven't you heard?

HATTIE. No. What news?

AMY LEE. Elizabeth surely you know.

HATTIE. No she doesn't.

AMY LEE. Oh, you must.

HATTIE. I tell you she doesn't!

AMY LEE. How do you know?

HATTIE. Because if she knew, she'd tell me, and then I'd know. But she didn't, so I don't, what news? (*Dramatic pause.*)

AMY LEE. Bridge is on the way out.

HATTIE. (*Crushed.*) Oh God!

AMY LEE. There is a new game.

HATTIE. Is it hard?

AMY LEE. It is an Oriental parlor game.

HATTIE. Is it harder than bridge?

ELIZABETH. What's the name of it.

AMY LEE. I'm sure it's going to be the new rage.

ELIZABETH. What's its name?

HATTIE. But, I just got through learning bridge!!

ELIZABETH. Hattie, hush up, what's its name, Amy.

AMY LEE. (*Pause.*) Mah jongg.

HATTIE. Mah jongg.

ELIZABETH. Mah jongg. (*Pause.*) I've heard of that game.

HATTIE. (*Scared.*) Well, I haven't.

AMY LEE. Trudy Stevens just came back from Dallas and she bought a mah jongg set at Neiman-Marcus.

ELIZABETH. That sounds like Trudy . . .

HATTIE. (*To Elizabeth.*) Don't you just know it's gonna be hard.

ELIZABETH. Calm down, we don't know anything about this game except it's Oriental. It might not be bad.

HATTIE. I'm real good at Chinese checkers.

ELIZABETH. See there.

AMY LEE. This is nothing like Chinese checkers. Mah jongg is a cultured parlor game that has been around for thousands of years.

HATTIE. See? They've had all that time to make it even harder!

ELIZABETH. Settle down! You don't know if it's going to be hard.

AMY LEE. It is *very* hard.

HATTIE. I knew it!

AMY LEE. Even Trudy Stevens can't figure it out. And she does comparative shopping!

ELIZABETH. Hattie, you're getting worked up over nothing.

AMY LEE. You mustn't let it upset you so.

HATTIE. I'm not upset! How do you play this game?

AMY LEE. It's played with tiles.

HATTIE. Tiles? Bathroom tiles?

AMY LEE. No, silly, with ivory tiles. Like dominoes. Only instead of little dots each tile represents a different style of tile. Like one tile will be four bamboos or three winds, or five dragons. Then you pass to your left, then you pass to your right, then, of course, there's your courtesy pass, a whirlwind of excitement! Then you want to build your wall.

HATTIE. (*Rising panic.*) Stop! I ain't building nothing. Bamboos, winds, dragons. It's no good. It took me a year to learn bridge. I concentrated my entire being on bridge. I neglected my house-work. My children nearly starved all for bridge which I finally learned. But I can't do it again. I can't go through that hell again. It'd kill me.

AMY LEE. Well, of course if you don't want to learn the game, you won't be able to play.

HATTIE. Shut up! I'll play if I want to.

31

AMY LEE. You won't play if you don't know the rules.

HATTIE. I'll know the rules 'cause we're still gonna play bridge. We're not changing games in midstream.

ELIZABETH. Hattie . . .

AMY LEE. What are you talking about?

HATTIE. I know what you're doing! You're trying to pull a fast one. You and Trudy Stevens are the only two that know the rules. You're trying to get us all to play this stupid game so you two can clean up!

AMY LEE. We are not!

HATTIE. You just want to be a couple of mah jongg hustlers. I know for a fact you and her cheat at bridge.

AMY LEE. We what!?

HATTIE. What'd you come over here for?

AMY LEE. To give Elizabeth this. (*Amy Lee picks up box. Hattie snatches box.*)

HATTIE. Yes, and what is this! I've been wanting to know all afternoon . . . (*Gasps.*) Is this mah jongg! (*Gasps.*) Are these the *tiles!* God they're big!!

AMY LEE. Those aren't the tiles.

HATTIE. Well, what's in here.

ELIZABETH. An air filter!

HATTIE. What's all this got to do with an Oriental parlor game?

AMY LEE. Nothing! Absolutely nothing! God you're stupid! You're an idiot! You're as stupid as that husband of yours and he's a moron.

HATTIE. Are you calling me a moron?

AMY LEE. No you're just an idiot. He's the moron.

ELIZABETH. Shut up, Amy Lee!

HATTIE. Watch what you say about Vernon Dealing. He's twice the man Skeeter Fullernoy is.

AMY LEE. They don't call him Skeeter no more.

HATTIE. Everybody calls him Skeeter.

AMY LEE. He may have been Skeeter once. But he's married to me now and he ain't never gonna be Skeeter again.

HATTIE. How come?

AMY LEE. Because of the appliance store, the chamber of commerce, and the country club, that's how come!

HATTIE. Oh yeah? Well I'm breaking into that country club next year!

AMY LEE. Huh! You and what army?

HATTIE. You can't keep me out!

AMY LEE. What makes you think I can't?

HATTIE. Why you little bitch!

ELIZABETH. Calm down both of you!

HATTIE. She can't talk to me that way! We grew up together, Amy Lee Braddley! Your folks were just as poor as mine!

AMY LEE. Yes but at least my Daddy wasn't a sharecropper.

HATTIE. Yeah, well at least I didn't marry for money.

AMY LEE. (*All cards on the table.*) Yes. I married Skeeter Fullernoy! And I've done all right for myself. I'm in the country club aren't I? There's nobody eligible in this stupid town, we all know that. Wayne Wilder was the best thing that ever happened to you. And he was a car thief!

ELIZABETH. Amy Lee!

AMY LEE. Wayne Wilder jilted you, you married Vernon and then you had a kid right off the bat. That always seemed funny to me!

HATTIE. (*Pause.*) Take that back.

AMY LEE. I don't have to.

HATTIE. You do if you want to stay healthy. (*Hattie advances on Amy Lee. Hattie begins to chase Amy Lee about the stage, first around the table grouping R., then around the table L., knocking chairs, props, etc., over as they go. Elizabeth follows them trying to intercede, Hattie and Amy Lee screaming all the while.*)

AMY LEE. Hattie! Hattie!

HATTIE. You little bitch.

AMY LEE. Oh Lord! Lord! (*Finally, Elizabeth manages to restrain Hattie, at which point Amy Lee begrudgingly speaks.*) OK. I'm sorry. (*Hiccups.*) I apologize. (*Hiccups.*) Oh God.

ELIZABETH. What is it?

AMY LEE. I got the hiccups. (*Hiccups.*)

ELIZABETH. You sure?

AMY LEE. (*Hiccups.*) Yes. (*Hiccups.*)

ELIZABETH. C'mon in the kitchen. (*Elizabeth takes her inside. Hattie follows, pauses in doorway.*)

HATTIE. (*Calling after them.*) They say best way to cure the hiccups is to scare someone. (*Hattie follows Amy Lee and Elizabeth into kitchen. We hear a tremendous scream from Hattie followed by much commotion.*)

AMY LEE. Oooooh.

ELIZABETH. Look what you've done. (*Amy Lee and Elizabeth come back onstage to retrieve Amy Lee's purse.*)

AMY LEE. Oh my God!

ELIZABETH. It's OK, Amy. It's OK.

AMY LEE. I want to go home.

ELIZABETH. Sure you don't want to—

AMY LEE. No home. (*Sweetly.*) I want to thank you for a real nice day.

ELIZABETH. You're sure you're OK.

AMY LEE. I'm fine. Perfectly fine. (*She sways a bit.*) Well, bye bye.

ELIZABETH. Bye bye, Amy Lee. (*Elizabeth exits with Amy Lee to see her to her car. Hattie comes onstage holding one of her shoes. She sits on the table.*)

AMY LEE. (*Off.*) Thank you for buying tickets to the pancake supper.

ELIZABETH. (*Off.*) Thank you, Amy. (*Elizabeth enters, sits in chair L.*).

HATTIE. Well. It's been a great day. My daughter was nearly arrested for shoplifting. My eldest son set fire to my mother-in-law's pekinese—and now a Baptist has barfed on my shoe. (*Pause. The two women chuckle together.*) Damn that's a pretty sunset.

ELIZABETH. Yeah, it's my favorite time.

HATTIE. That's one thing Texas is good for—sunsets.

ELIZABETH. It's the only time things get soft. (*Pause.*) Look, Hattie. The evening star. (*Pause.*)

HATTIE. That was quick thinking about Margaret Crowell.

ELIZABETH. Hattie.

HATTIE. Huh?

ELIZABETH. I'm sorry it never worked out for you and Wayne.

HATTIE. What's that supposed to mean?

ELIZABETH. I think that's what we've been talking about all afternoon. Roy and I. Wayne and you.

HATTIE. Hell no. That's all over with years ago. I'm better off with old Vernon. He isn't worth kicking off the porch . . . but we're, well, comfortable together . . . Now, Wayne was . . . he was too . . . hell, Wayne was Wayne . . . Sure, I loved him. You bet. (*Pause.*)

ELIZABETH. Well I love Roy, Hattie, and he needs me right now. He doesn't know it. But he does. (*Pause.*) And I'm going to be here. (*Pause.*)

HATTIE. (*Standing.*) Well, I gotta go get the kids.

ELIZABETH. OK.

HATTIE. Never did finish folding your laundry.

ELIZABETH. I'll get to it. (*Pause. The women stand facing each other.*

*Hattie unconsciously touches Elizabeth's stomach. They smile, then pull away.)*

HATTIE. You hang onto Roy.

ELIZABETH. I intend to.

HATTIE. He's the last wild thing left around here. (*Pause.*) Talk to you tomorrow?

ELIZABETH. Yeah. Call me. (*Hattie exits. Elizabeth turns on phonograph again. As the lights fade to black, Elizabeth takes a deep breath. Blackout.*)

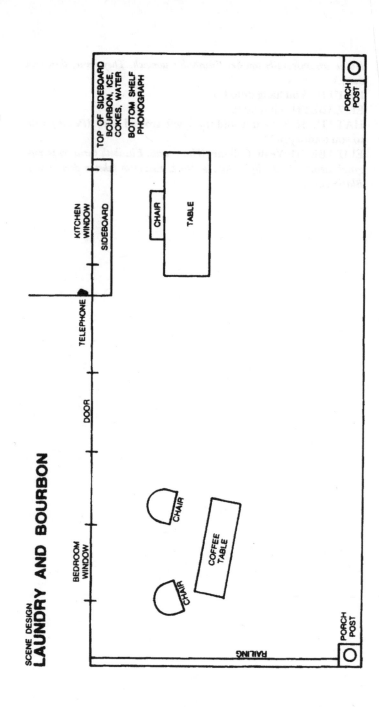

SCENE DESIGN
**LAUNDRY AND BOURBON**

PORCH POST

TOP OF SIDEBOARD
BOURBON, ICE,
COKES, WATER

BOTTOM SHELF
PHONOGRAPH

KITCHEN WINDOW

SIDEBOARD

TELEPHONE

CHAIR

TABLE

DOOR

BEDROOM WINDOW

CHAIR

CHAIR

COFFEE TABLE

PORCH POST

RAILING

# PROPERTY PLOT

*Onstage:*
   Ceiling fan
   Two rocking chairs
   Coffee table
   Laundry basket with unfolded laundry, including man's T-shirts, boxer
      shorts, shirt with pearl buttons, bedsheet
   Magazines and newspapers
   Sideboard with bottle of bourbon, ice, cokes, water, glasses
   Black telephone
   Portable record player
   Kitchen table
   One kitchen chair
   Television set on wooden crate
*Offstage* (kitchen):
   Tray with crackers, avocado dip, etc. (Elizabeth)
   Purse with $5 (Elizabeth)
*Personal:*
   Elizabeth—cigarette, book
   Hattie—floral print dress, wristwatch, purse containing make-up and
      checkbook
   Amy Lee—floral print dress (same as Hattie's), large unmarked box,
      purse containing roll of tickets
*SOUND EFFECTS*
   Doorbell
   Phone ringing

# NEW PLAYS

★ **A DELICATE SHIP by Anna Ziegler.** A haunting love triangle triggers an unexpected chain of events in this poetic play. In the early stages of a new relationship, Sarah and Sam are lovers happily discovering each other. Sarah and Nate know everything about each other, best of friends since childhood and maybe something more. But when Nate shows up unannounced on Sarah's doorstep, she's left questioning what and who she wants in this humorous and heartbreaking look at love, memory, and the decisions that alter the course of our lives. "Ziegler (who makes origami of time)… digs beneath the laughs, of which there are plenty, to plumb the pain that lurks below." –*Time Out (NY)*. [2M, 1W] ISBN: 978-0-8222-3453-1

★ **HAND TO GOD by Robert Askins.** After the death of his father, meek Jason finds an outlet for his anxiety at the Christian Puppet Ministry, in the devoutly religious, relatively quiet small town of Cypress, Texas. Jason's complicated relationships with the town pastor, the school bully, the girl next door, and—most especially—his mother are thrown into upheaval when Jason's puppet, Tyrone, takes on a shocking and dangerously irreverent personality all its own. HAND TO GOD explores the startlingly fragile nature of faith, morality, and the ties that bind us. "HAND TO GOD is so ridiculously raunchy, irreverent and funny it's bound to leave you sore from laughing. Ah, hurts so good." –*NY Daily News*. [3M, 2W] ISBN: 978-0-8222-3292-6

★ **PLATONOV by Anton Chekhov, translated by John Christopher Jones.** PLATONOV is Chekhov's first play, and it went unproduced during his lifetime. Finding himself on a downward spiral fueled by lust and alcohol, Platonov proudly adopts as his motto "speak ill of everything." A shining example of the chaos that reigned in his era, Platonov is a Hamlet whose father was never murdered, a Don Juan who cheats on his wife and his mistress, and the hero of the as-yet unwritten great Russian novel of his day. [9M, 4W] ISBN: 978-0-8222-3343-5

★ **JUDY by Max Posner.** It's the winter of 2040, and the world has changed—but maybe not by much. Timothy's wife has just left him, and he isn't taking it well. His sisters, Tara and Kris, are trying to help him cope while wrestling with their own lives and loves. The three of them seem to spend a lot of time in their basements, and the kids are starting to ask questions. This subterranean comedy explores how one family hangs on when technology fails and communication breaks down. "This smart, disturbing comedy is set…just far enough in the future to be intriguingly weird but close enough to the present to be distressingly familiar… Posner's revelations about this brave new world… waver between the explicit and the mysterious, and each scene… gives us something funny and scary to ponder." –*The New Yorker*. [3M, 3W] ISBN: 978-0-8222-3462-3

**DRAMATISTS PLAY SERVICE, INC.**
440 Park Avenue South, New York, NY 10016 212-683-8960
postmaster@dramatists.com  www.dramatists.com

# NEW PLAYS

★ **PLACEBO by Melissa James Gibson.** A minty green pill—medication or sugar? Louise is working on a placebo-controlled study of a new female arousal drug. As her work in the lab navigates the blurry lines between perception and deception, the same questions pertain more and more to her life at home. With uncanny insight and unparalleled wit, Melissa James Gibson's affectionate comedy examines slippery truths and the power of crossed fingers. "Smart, droll, beautifully observed…" *–New York Magazine.* "… subtle yet intellectually explosive…" *–TheaterMania.com.* [2M, 2W] ISBN: 978-0-8222-3369-5

★ **THE ROAD TO DAMASCUS by Tom Dulack.** As full-scale civil war rages in Syria, a bomb explodes in Manhattan and all roads lead to Damascus. A peace-seeking African Pope is elected to the Vatican and an Evangelical third-party president is in power in the U.S. With nuclear war looming, will the new Pope intervene directly in American foreign policy, or will he accede to the demands of Washington? Riddled with international intrigue, Tom Dulack's astonishingly prescient play imagines a world ripped from today's headlines. "Serious… satisfying… This near-future tale of an ill-conceived American plan feels authentic enough to have you believe that such events could take place any day. Or to remind you that similar ones have already occurred." *–NY Times.* [5M, 2W] ISBN: 978-0-8222-3407-4

★ **FOUR PLACES by Joel Drake Johnson.** When Peggy's two adult children take her out for lunch, they quietly begin to take apart her life. The drinks come fast, the tempers peak, the food flies. "… a meticulously structured work that captures a decades-long history of paralyzing family resentments, depleted affections, and sublimated cruelties in a single, uninterrupted 90-minute scene." *–Chicago Reader.* "FOUR PLACES is intense, remorseless drama at its finest." *–Backstage.* [1M, 3W] ISBN: 978-0-8222-3448-7

★ **THE BIRDS by Conor McPherson, from a story by Daphne du Maurier.** The short story that inspired Alfred Hitchcock's classic film is boldly adapted by Conor McPherson—a gripping, unsettling, and moving look at human relationships in the face of societal collapse. In an isolated house, strangers Nat and Diane take shelter from relentless masses of attacking birds. They find relative sanctuary but not comfort or peace; there's no electricity, little food, and a nearby neighbor may still be alive and watching them. Another refugee, the young and attractive Julia, arrives with some news of the outside world, but her presence also brings discord. Their survival becomes even more doubtful when paranoia takes hold of the makeshift fortress—an internal threat to match that of the birds outside. "Deliciously chilling… spring-loaded with tension…" *–Irish Independent.* "[McPherson] keeps us on the edge of our seat." *–Irish Times.* [2M, 2W] ISBN: 978-0-8222-3312-1

**DRAMATISTS PLAY SERVICE, INC.**
440 Park Avenue South, New York, NY 10016 212-683-8960
postmaster@dramatists.com  www.dramatists.com

# NEW PLAYS

★ **BUZZER by Tracey Scott Wilson.** Jackson, an upwardly-mobile black attorney, has just bought an apartment in a transitioning neighborhood in Brooklyn. He sees the potential of his old neighborhood, as does his white girlfriend Suzy… at first. When Jackson's childhood friend Don leaves rehab to crash with them, the trio quickly becomes trapped between the tensions inside their own home and the dangers that may lurk outside. "Skillful… [a] slow-burning, thought-provoking drama…" –*NY Times.* "[In BUZZER,] race is not a national conversation but an inner turmoil… the fact that the main gentrifier here is black turns the usual view of the subject inside out: Can one gentrify one's own home?" –*New York Magazine.* [3M, 1W] ISBN: 978-0-8222-3411-1

★ **THE NANCE by Douglas Carter Beane.** In the 1930s, burlesque impresarios welcomed the hilarious comics and musical parodies of vaudeville to their decidedly lowbrow niche. A headliner called "the nance"—usually played by a straight man—was a stereotypically camp homosexual and master of comic double entendre. THE NANCE recreates the naughty, raucous world of burlesque's heyday and tells the backstage story of Chauncey Miles and his fellow performers. At a time when it was easy to play gay and dangerous to be gay, Chauncey's uproarious antics on the stage stand out in marked contrast to his offstage life. "A nearly perfect work of dramatic art…" –*The New Yorker.* [4M, 4W] ISBN: 978-0-8222-3077-9

★ **EMPANADA LOCA by Aaron Mark.** Now living deep under Manhattan in an abandoned subway tunnel with the Mole People, a very hungry Dolores recounts her years selling weed with her boyfriend, her return to Washington Heights after thirteen years in prison, her fortuitous reunion with an old stoner friend who lets her give massages for cash in the basement under his empanada shop, and the bloodbath that sent her fleeing underground. Loosely inspired by the legend of Sweeney Todd, EMPANADA LOCA is contemporary Grand Guignol horror in the style of Spalding Gray. "Exuberantly macabre…" –*NY Times.* "Spine-tingling and stomach-churning…" –*Time Out (NY).* [1W] ISBN: 978-0-8222-3476-0

★ **SENSE OF AN ENDING by Ken Urban.** Charles, a discredited *New York Times* journalist, arrives in Rwanda for an exclusive interview with two Hutu nuns. Charged with alleged war crimes committed during the 1994 genocide, the nuns must convince the world of their innocence or face a lifetime in prison. When an unknown Tutsi survivor contradicts their story, Charles must choose which version of the truth to tell. Based on real events, SENSE OF AN ENDING shines a light on questions of guilt, complicity, and faith in the face of extreme violence. "A superb play… so intense that, in between each scene, you can hear the audience gulp for air." –*Time Out (London).* [3M, 2W] ISBN: 978-0-8222-3094-6

**DRAMATISTS PLAY SERVICE, INC.**
440 Park Avenue South, New York, NY 10016 212-683-8960
postmaster@dramatists.com  www.dramatists.com